The College of Hip Hop.org Presents:
Ten Steps to Profit
From your Passion

Dedication

This book is dedicated to the memory of LaVell A. Jackson Jr. You are and have always been our greatest musical influence. Rest peacefully, cousin

CONTENTS

Introduction
1. Invest in Your Dreams
2. Setting Goals
3. Creating a Budget
4. Five Rules for Monetizing Your Music
5. What Is a Tax ID Number and Do You Need One for Your Label
6. Types of Record Deals (P and D, 360, Artist, Production Level
7. Recording Contracts 101
8. Importance of Good Packaging
9. Street Team – Making the Music Is the Easy Part
10. Creating Viral Content

Acknowledgments

Introduction

The ride home from the Ohio Hip Hop Awards to Michigan was a lot different than the ride there. No music, just my brother and I bouncing ideas off each other for the next few hours.

"How can we get booked to sit on the panel?" asked SJ.

"What is the culture missing that we can bring to it?" was my answer.

"What don't the artists seem to know that we can TEACH them?" was his reply.

As we drove home, the ideas continued to flow. When we pulled into his driveway to drop him off at home, still NOTHING had been agreed upon, or even billed as a "good idea", for that matter. As I drove home, eager to see my family (it had been a long weekend), the ideas continued to flow during my ride. We both had thought of some things, but what could WE do to be innovative and change the way artists approach the BUSINESS of entertainment and music? Once home, my first call was to SJ.

"Did you come up with anything yet?"

"No; still thinking."

"Me, too. I'll let you know tomorrow if something comes up."

"Okay. Love you, bro. Talk to you tomorrow."

And that was it. A music conference filled with artists and they all wanted the same thing: to be signed to a major label—well, any label for that matter—and our approach throughout our career is to stay independent, gain ownership, and LEARN the business because, after all, that's what it is—"SHOW BUSINESS!" While those thoughts crowded my brain, I decided to take a shower to relax. Then it dawned on me, *We need to teach the artists and the aspiring CEOs the business of music.*'

I immediately called my brother, and before I could tell him what I had just thought of, he said, "I got it! We need to teach the artists ownership and the business side of the industry."

"I was just about to say the same thing to you."

At that exact moment, *The College of Hip Hop.org* was born.

What is *The College of Hip Hop.org?*

Over the past decades, the only thing that has remained consistent in the arts and entertainment industry is the business aspect. The purpose of www.TheCollegeOfHipHop.org is to teach the business aspect of arts and entertainment to aspiring talent and CEOs. The knowledge gained from becoming a paid subscriber will empower CEOs and the talent to understand and value the arts and entertainment industry more.

The College of Hip Hop.org is the premier online learning institution, which uses dynamic seminars to educate our students on key elements of the arts and entertainment business. You will learn such fundamentals as:

- How to start a publishing company;
- How to copyright and encode your music;
- Vocal training and choreography; and
- Other industry-related topics.

1. Invest In Your Dreams

We're told to follow our dreams at an early age. The world is our oyster and we relish in what could be. Our dream is where we see ourselves in the future. It's where we want to be as far as a career or our field of interest. Most people know what they want to be, but they don't posses the mentality it takes to make their dreams come true—that is, the will to invest in their dreams.

Growing up in a family full of boys, I've seen them go from being stellar athletes to rappers. They would go to the studio and write, then rap over a beat produced by my cousin. Of course, this encouraged others to test their skills on the mic. My youngest brother wanted to rap as well. They wouldn't let him rap with them, for some reason I am not sure of.

My brother didn't allow them to stop him. He ventured out on his own and found a studio. He recorded two songs and said to me, "Kiya, you want to hear my songs?"

Of course I listened, and soon enough, the whole house heard his music. Everyone was astonished. I was proud. I saw in him a go-getter attitude. He showed everyone the talent they'd refused to let flourish. Since I knew about his grind and work ethic, I personally invested in him. I paid for his studio time, I vouched for him, and I set up platforms so he could be seen—all because he showed me he was willing to make things work for himself.

He asked me one day if I thought he could make it in music. All I could say was, "You are willing to do what others aren't. They say no, you keep working—you write every day, you invest in your music, you're even willing to get a job to help pay for studio time! That sounds like the character of somebody who will make it."

The point is, if you want people to invest in your dreams, invest in yourself first!

Some things to think about:

1. Identify your dreams via a vision board.
2. What steps can you take to turn your dreams to reality?

2. Setting Goals

"Where do you see yourself in two years?"

That is a question you should take into deep consideration. This is where goal-setting comes into play. Goals can be interpreted in two different ways. Your goal can be the actual "PRIZE" you seek to obtain, or it can be the steps taken to reach the "PRIZE". I view both as goals because the meaning is interchangeable. One thing to keep in mind, the difference between goals and a to-do list is deadlines. Goals work together to reach a prize, while with a to-do list, you're completing tasks.

Setting goals is possible. Let's say you want to lower your blood sugar. It should be your daily goal to decrease your starch intake. Why? Starch breaks down into sugar, and your blood sugar is your issue. If you want to lower your blood sugar, you must first decrease your sugar and starch intake.

In life, to even chase after our dreams, we must set goals. If you don't set goals, you will run around in circles with no direction and everyone will notice. The first step in setting goals is determining the "PRIZE" you're after, or the dream you're chasing. Next, make a list of steps or goals you believe will help you reach the "ULTIMATE GOAL", in other words the "PRIZE". Below is an example of the goals of an artist's manager when completing certain projects.

The main goal or the "PRIZE" in this particular case is to make sure the artist has a successful EP (a five-to-eight song album). This is just an example of the goals that may be set.

- Brainstorm and create a vision for my artist's EP. Have a clear understanding of the EP's theme and aesthetics by **October 15.**

- Ensure the artist has everything needed to create music. Make sure the artist has pens, notebooks, and other items to ensure he/she is comfortable and ready to make music by **October 16.**

- Book studio time for the next two months by **October 20.**

- Lockdown features from artist on the project who will create borrowed interest for my artist, **October 21-November 1.**

- Get a graphic designer by **November 5.**

Some things to think about:

1. Rationalize your goals.
2. Set time frame for achieving your goals.
3. Expand on your goals

3. Creating a Budget

You've heard it said, "It takes money to make money." This is especially true in the entertainment industry. But how much money does it take to *make it*?

Whenever you look to work with someone on a higher level in this business, you'll be asked, "What is your budget?" If you say, "I don't have one," often you'll end up parting ways. They may assume you don't have money to spend, but in reality, it may mean you don't understand how to CREATE a budget in the first place. That's where we want to help you. We want to help you learn how much you need to set aside so when you're asked, "What's your budget?" you'll have an intelligent answer.

The most important part of setting a budget is determining your goals. What is it you want to accomplish? Do you want to record an album? Go on tour? Print merchandise? What expenses can arise from that?

If you want to create an album, what expenses are associated with that? Where will you record? In your room? Do you have all the equipment already? If not, what do you need and how much does it cost? If you want to use a professional studio, what is their hourly rate and how much time do you need to record? Make sure you have your lyrics memorized, so when you're in the studio, you can just lay down vocals and move on, which will save you time and money.

Do you produce yourself, or buy or lease beats? How much is that? How much is it to mix and master? How much are copyrights? You need to research every possible cost from services to travel expenses to shipping-and-handling costs. These are all part of your budget.

You have to want to do more than just make music if you want to succeed in this business. Obviously an educated team is needed to really make moves, but if you aren't familiar with the basics, it is easy to be taken advantage of and to make mistakes. Knowledge is power.

Some things to think about:

1. Create a realistic budget.
2. Stick to your budget.
3. Once your revenue starts to increase, increase your budget for the next project.

4. Five Rules for Monetizing Your Music

Regardless of how much you make music for the "love of the art", you release it publicly because you want to make money from it. A big part of declining music sales can be attributed to the availability of music for free. In the last fifteen-plus years, the idea you should build anticipation for your album by giving music away has run rampant. You must always set the expectation that your music is for sale. And when it isn't, you have to make a way to generate income.

Rule 1:   *Give the consumer the option.*

Some people will buy your mixtape even though it's free if they had an opportunity. Print physical copies and take them to local stores to be sold. Also make them available on digital stores for those you may not be able to reach with a physical copy.

Rule 2:   *Merchandise*

Much like making CDs to sell or even give away, having merchandise can help in several ways. If you sell the items, they are automatically an advertisement for you, spreading awareness of your project. Depending on what types of items you create, this can be costly up front, but if properly executed, the money will make itself back and then some. Also, if the music is given in a package with the merchandise, you can possibly count those as album sales.

Rule 3:   *Register Your Music*

A lot of money an artist, especially an independent, makes can come from spins, streams, and views. You must join one of the performance-rights organizations in order to get paid. Even if you aren't getting radio play, but your music is being played on other outlets registered for licensing—be it online or TV—you can make money. If you don't have an affiliation with one of the performance-rights groups, you won't be paid.

Rule 4: Placements

Long before you break out as a star, you can get big checks by having your music on movies, TV, video games, and more. The easiest way to accomplish this is by having an agent. They can get your music to the music directors for other media outlets and shop for placements. With placement on less-traditional outlets, you can reach more people organically and make money at the same time—without as much legwork.

Rule 5: Features

Once you build enough momentum and become in demand, you can start charging for feature verses on other artists' songs. Much like the other rules, these guest appearances expand your brand and make you money. Unlike some of the others, this usually won't cost you anything.

With so many online outlets giving away music, artists have conformed. When mixtape started out as a tool to expose an artist, it was usually full of remixes to already popular songs and only a few originals. Now, what would have been an album in the golden era and sold commercially is free to anyone interested in it. Some artists have given away much more than they even have available to buy. To offset the low sales, artists branch off into other revenue streams as discussed in these steps and more.

Some things to think about:

1. What are the five most important elements of your music career?

2. Can you PROFIT from your five most important elements of your music career?

5. What Is a Tax ID Number and Do You Need One for Your Label

If you pay attention to the media, taxes and hip hop don't seem to be good friends. How many stories have you heard about big stars who owe back-taxes? How many times have I gone to events and artists didn't realize they could write-off the mileage, food, and hotel for the events on their taxes?

We file our taxes using our social security numbers, but businesses use what's called an EIN, Employer Identification Number. It's basically an ID number used and given by the U.S. federal government to businesses for tax purposes and other filings with the government.

The default category if you haven't filed as a corporation or an LLC (Limited Liability Company) is what's called a Sole Proprietorship, which means you are only the owner (sole proprietor). If that's the case, you can just use your personal social security number for your taxes, and you don't need to apply for a separate number.

Say I want to start ESSINCE PRODUCTIONS. I'm the only owner and the only artist for the time being, but I want to protect my personal assets in case of a lawsuit somewhere down the road, and I decide to incorporate my company or make it an LLC (this is also true for partnerships). Then I *will* need to apply for a tax ID number. Even though I'm the only owner and worker, the government sees my business entity as a separate person, so I'll need a separate tax ID number. If I'm going to hire employees, then I'll need a new tax ID number.

You also may not want to use your personal social security number every time you apply for a business credit card, or if you're hired as an independent contractor for a project, some companies may want you to have one so it doesn't appear that you're their employee.

Luckily, applying for a tax ID number is free and easy. There is a simple form on the IRS website: https://sa.www4.irs.gov/modiein/individual/index.jsp. You will get your tax ID number immediately. Your tax status doesn't change and you don't have to pay extra taxes just for having one, but it makes your filing easier when you separate personal and business matters.

Some things to think about:

1. Why are tax IDs so important?
2. Should you get a tax ID?
3. How can a tax ID help your business?

6. Types of Record Deals
(P and D, 360, Artist, Production Deal)

A common misconception is all deals offered by major labels are the now (incorrectly?) infamous "360". A 360 doesn't have to be seen as a negative. Remember, there is no such thing as a "standard agreement" in the music business, and the terms are negotiable. However, if you don't have a lot of independent success, your leveraging power isn't strong, and you may not be offered the best options.

The question you need to ask yourself is, "What do I want from the music business?"

If your biggest concern is creative control, but you still want to be seen on a national scale, then a distribution deal might be better. Or maybe you want to work directly with a top producer or artist and sign under his/her label, instead of directly with a major label (for example, Aftermath instead of directly with Interscope).

Perhaps you want to be seen worldwide and be on TV, radio, and more! Major or independent labels can still be structured the same way. If an indie label has dreams of being bought out, they'll have major label structuring to their agreements. It's important to know what you're getting into and the types of deals so you can make an educated choice. Let's start with the most well known, the misunderstood "360" deal.

Let's say you're an independent artist who has achieved regional success. You do shows and can bring a solid crowd, and you're now able to sell about 10,000 albums. (Sales numbers are down but a large majority of urban music sales are STILL from physical CDs, despite what you read, but I digress.) With those 10,000 sales, show money, and merchandise, you are bringing in around $100,000 a year. If a major label comes to you and offers $400,000, wouldn't you entertain the idea or at least hear them out?

The **360 Deal** means the label will earn a percentage of every facet of your career—album sales, merchandise, touring, and sponsorships. That sounds unfair to artists, right? But from the label's point of view, if I'm giving you a few hundred thousand dollars and using my connections to get you national media exposure, headlining international tours, and thousands of new fans, I want a portion of everything. Your manager gets a percentage, right? You can negotiate the rates.

Another common option is a **Production Deal,** and no, it's not just for producers, but you may be working directly *with* a producer. Production deals are arguably the closest to development deals we still have. An artist will sign directly with a producer or a small label. Generally, production labels don't have direct distribution, but it comes through the label if they are signed to one. If they haven't secured distribution, then an artist on a production label will be developed and the demos produced will be shopped to labels.

Lastly, we'll discuss the **Pressing and Distribution Deal**. Many production labels have what is called a P&D deal, in which the distributor will manufacture and ship the albums to the stores for a commission (generally 25%). However, the labels signed to a deal like this are competing with the other labels being distributed, much like artists on a label are competing with other acts to sell music.

Some things to think about:

1. Will a record deal help or hurt you?
2. What type of record deal would work best for you?
3. Do you understand the difference in the types of record deals?

7. Recording Contracts 101

If you're reading this, that means you're ready to move on to the next stage in your music career—the DEAL! Someone believes enough in you to offer you an agreement. So what should you expect to see in a contract?

FIRST, I can't stress this enough: ***PLEASE*** get an entertainment lawyer to read any and all agreements. Not your cousin who's a divorce lawyer, an ***ENTERTAINMENT LAWYER***. If your kid had bronchitis, would you go to a proctologist? No, right? So why would you not speak with an ENTERTAINMENT lawyer about your music legal needs?

Second, I want you to remember, there are no such things as "standard" agreements. What I mean by that is a new artist agreement SHOULD have *similarities* from all labels, and there will likely be templates the legal teams use to craft agreements for each label, but an offer from Universal for a new artist will be different from an offer from Atlantic for what appears to be the same deal. And I want you to remember that contracts are negotiable. Just because you're offered something doesn't usually mean it's this or nothing. The back-and-forth can take some time.

With this, you need to have an understanding of the budget you're given to create your album and the percentages offered so you'll understand your earnings!

What **PERCENTAGE** will you [hopefully] be paid? Usually on a major label, you'll be offered around twelve percent (12%) of albums SOLD on your first album. SOLD is not the same as SHIPPED, but that's another lesson. Look at WHAT RATE you'll be paid and also WHEN you'll be paid. If you're given an advance (money up front), how much in sales do you need to generate until you start earning money?

If you're given a $200,000 advance, that needs to go toward expenses of the album. Many deals will give another $300,000 for promotion, totaling a $500,000 deal, referred to as your 'aggregate sum' (aka 'debt' you need to repay). That's an easy number to work with for these examples. This will be your **BUDGET**.

So from that $200,000 (remember, the rest goes to promotion), you are responsible for creating the album, video, hiring producers, working in studios and more. If you have a manager who takes a 15% commission, then the $200,000 now becomes $170,000. Unless you paid your lawyer up front, she/he will take a negotiation fee now, so $5,000 seems reasonable. You are now left with $165,000. Now you want to work with the hottest producer in the game, right? Well, this producer wants $20,000 to produce your album (not just a beat maker; it can be someone to make beats, also find features, help craft the sound of the album, develop, etc.). Your $200,000 advance is now down to $145,000 before you've even stepped foot in the studio!

Right Way vs. Wrong Way

You're signed now! You're a success, right? Time to buy the big house, fancy cars, and jewelry, right? You have $145,000! You blow it all and have nothing left to record your album. No album = no sales. No sales = no way to repay, and your career is OVER. ***OR*** you can be smart and put your money into making the best project you can. But if you spend the whole budget in the studio, hopefully you have other money stashed away, because that budget is the only money you'll get from the record label until you've repaid them!

So you decide to keep your costs low and set aside money to live on. Smart! But remember this money is all pre-taxes! Maybe you'll work with up-n-coming artists and beat makers, and will be able to record in a cheap studio.

You should set aside money for unexpected expenses. Life happens and you need to be sure you have extra money to finish your album and live on. You decide to spend $80,000 making your album, and set aside $20,000 for emergencies.

Now let's recap and put all the math into perspective.

You're offered a half-million-dollar deal! You agree that the label can spend $300,000 in promotion and $200,000 goes to you.

$200,000 - $30,000 (manager) - $5,000 (lawyer)   = $165,000

$165,000 - $20,000 (producer)   = $145,000

$145,000 - $80,000 (album budget)   = $65,000

$65,000 - $20,000 (emergencies)   = $45,000

for you . . . unless you're in a group—then it's time to split that up . . . then pay taxes.

Now before you get too scared, remember once you release your single/album, hopefully you'll be earning show money, setting up endorsements, and you'll be bringing in money from publishing as well. So, there are other ways to generate money, but that's why you need an excellent manager to set up these ventures for you.

Some things to think about:

1. Should I have a lawyer look over my contract?
2. Who should negotiate contracts on my behalf?

8. Importance of Good Packaging

Every day someone is dropping a mixtape and it's the HOTTEST EVER! The biggest DJ hosts it and they're about to flood the streets. With music (especially hip hop) being so saturated, the difference between a win and a loss could be something as simple as presentation. Your cover art or disc labeling could separate your project from the pack.

The presentation is key for anyone planning to sell a product. Quality materials add value to your album/mixtape. Proper packaging creates the perception that you have invested in the project and it will be worth the money. If you don't show you're serious about how your items look, people might conclude the music was also approached in the same way. People always judge—*even if they say they don't.*

How your packaging looks is your music's first impression on the consumers. It should draw eyes to the project on shelves and websites alike. Interesting artwork and CD printing may seem like an unimportant part of putting your mixtape/album out, but it is basically the first step to building interest in you to people you haven't directly approached or marketed to.

Using high-quality materials can extend your music's shelf-life long after you've moved on to something else. The wrong case or low-quality materials could be more damaging perceptually and leave the product more vulnerable to damage. Present your project professionally and increase the appeal to generate profit.

Some things to think about:

1. How do I make my packaging stand out from others?
2. How much should I allocate from my budget to packaging?

9. Street Team - Making the Music Is the Easy Part

Today's artists think by recording fifteen songs then putting them online, they can change their situation or status. Most never consider the hard work with various promotional tactics necessary to succeed. One of the most important marketing tools is the ability to breach your consumer's subconscious. Street team promotion is the method of supplying your target audience with various flyers, CDs, posters, etc., they can take with them. The hope is, when they come across the item you've given them, they'll remember the product you're promoting and take action on it.

Anyone trying to sell a product must first attract interest. Street teams are an easy way to accomplish that. Consider your product the same as a compelling rumor. One person tells someone, who then tells another, and so on. The street team promotional product is what starts the *"rumor"*. A single flyer can generate interest to countless people if you're able to get just one person to pass it on. Sometimes it takes one hundred flyers to get one person who passes it on and spreads the "rumor", but if it's being spread from multiple outlets, you increase the chances of it catching on.

Nowadays the "rumors" are only being spread to people who already know or only online. If you don't have a network of people who plant seeds all over, the product dies. Labels and independents alike have gotten lazy (and cheap). Street teams are essential in branding your music and setting the foundation for a lasting impact. Be prepared to spend money on promotional items and for hiring experienced street team workers to get the most impact per item circulating.

Def Jam. No Limit. Ruff Ryders. All these major successes were a hard sell to the mainstream world initially. Russell Simmons, Master P, and DMX are just a few examples of how organic growth can pay off BIG. Today's music industry is very digital, and in turn, less connected. The internet has and continues to revolutionize our day-to-day life, but human interaction has suffered because of it.

Russell Simmons and company changed music indefinitely when they started Def Jam. People were exposed to their artists in less-invasive ways and had the option to choose. He threw parties, handed out flyers, and plastered New York with posters. By strategically placing his products, he was able to win over the world. He promoted his artists in the same way they should be—as a campaign. The promotion of the artists was probably seen more than the artists themselves.

Master P had to go to California and start up a separate business to spread the "rumor". No one would sign DMX because of his roughness, but he built up his name by getting people to spread the "rumor". Becoming a star is like running for office—if people don't see the signs promoting you or hear about it from someone else, **YOU LOSE**. Making the music is just you applying for a candidacy.

Some things to think about:

1. Are street teams still relevant?
2. When is the right time to hire a street team?

10. Creating Viral Content

The term "viral", like many descriptive words nowadays, is grossly overused *and* misused. (Think "hilarious" or "amazing".) Using the word "viral" in a YouTube video title does not make a video viral. The views, votes, and comments tell me that by looking at your numbers, and if I hear about something outside of a music blog or YouTube-suggested videos, then I know you may be on to something.

Okay, so if it's not in the view numbers or the title, what makes something *viral*? Merriam-Webster defines viral as (1) *of, relating to, or caused by a virus (a* viral *infection)*, and (2) *quickly and widely spread or popularized especially by person-to-person electronic communication (a* viral *video)*. Viral, as pertaining to a VIRUS. The best way to understand it is to think of how easily germs are spread in an elementary school. One kid gets a cold, the flu, or lice? It spreads.

So how do you make people want to share something? Simple—*emotional content*. People love to share experiences, be they good or bad. *Make them react*. Ever eaten something disgusting and told someone else to try it? Ever seen the YouTube videos where something scary jumps up out of nowhere? People like to be scared. Make people connect to your content emotionally and they'll WANT to share it. There's nothing about sitting in a mansion with bags of cash that makes me send it to a friend like, "Yo, you have to see this!" But make me laugh, scream, throw up, or cry, and I'll tell everybody.

It's all about the content and the emotional connection you create with your fans.

❖ ❖ ❖

Some things to think about:

1. When will I know that my content has gone *viral?*
2. Do I need my content to go *viral* to be considered a "hit" artist?

Acknowledgments

The College of Hip Hip.org would like to acknowledge Brian "Essince" Collins, Karyn Shanks of Mean Girlz Media, and Kiya Hickman for being contributing writers for this project. We appreciate all of your time assisting us in building our company. Thank you: Kijuanna Jackson and Chauncey "Mr. Rain" Jackson, for steering us in the right direction; Kimmie Jackson, for being a great mom and always supporting our hustle; Ebonee and Aiyona Jackson, for keeping AJ on the right path; the Jackson, Legion, Prince, and Shearer families; and last but not least, every musical artist as well as aspiring CEO—past, present and future—who yearns to learn the business of music.

The College Of Hip Hop.org

Be sure to visit www.thecollegeofhiphop.org and become a paid subscriber to view all of our visual seminars and enhance your knowledge of the arts and entertainment industries.

If you would like to contact The College of Hip Hop.org with questions about the book, you can do so by email: questions@tcohh.org

www.ingramcontent.com/pod-product-compliance
Lightning Source LLC
Chambersburg PA
CBHW071804040426
42446CB00012B/2697